MW01121416

MOMENTS IN TIME

Poetry, 1993–2007

Hilary Thursfield

ARTHUR H. STOCKWELL LTD
Torrs Park   Ilfracombe   Devon
Established 1898
www.ahstockwell.co.uk

British Library Cataloguing-in-Publication Data.
A catalogue record for this book is available
from the British Library.

ISBN 978-0-7223-4043-1
Printed in Great Britain by
Arthur H. Stockwell Ltd
Torrs Park   Ilfracombe
Devon

Contents

If I Must Be an Old Lady

Let me be an eccentric one
Who still interacts with the young;
Let me tip my hat to strangers
When passing by a farmer's field;
Knock apples off trees with my stick,
So I still get a thrill from dangers;
And let me visit you on a raid
Wearing my deep purple and gold
So you can tell me once again
That I never could be so old.
And if I dance to fiddle and flute,
I hope you'll still think me cute
As my back buckles and gives out
And I begin to shout obscenities
At anyone who happens to be about
Just for the sheer fun of it.
And while immersed in my books
On some mystery or ancient art
I'll skip over the boring part
And do things old ladies don't do:
Smoke pot and hum Led Zeppelin,
Eat gum, blow bubbles and chew.
Let me make merry all alone
When no one calls on the phone;
Have fun with a silent repartee,
Just my imagination and me.
And if you call while I am out,
You know that I have surely been
Up to my ears in weird things

That ever an old man has seen.
Let me still fight for the oppressed
In this or some far-off land,
And if I don't carry the banner,
Wave you aside with my hand.
And if I should drop my shawl,
It's probably because I wish it gone
So don't buy me a new one.
A mental traveller now if you please,
Only if I have trouble with knees.
It is hard this growing old
When only half the tale is told;
And if I've forgotten the rest,
Make it up! Yes, you guessed.

Mexico

Oh, Mexico!
Your clouds hang loose over the mountains,
Become the roof of my dreams.
The Pacific Ocean lifts me, frees me
From bondage and anchors,
Leaves me light-headed and full
Of all life's possibilities.
Here I am energized,
A wild fervour to my step –
Walk like someone with a purpose
On your prized shores.
You show me beauty in your horizons.
On my palm-splattered canvas
Your colours have touched me, moved me;
I am renewed and reinvented.
I emerge enthused and aroused
As though I had been sleeping
For some long years;
I have surfaced with clarity and insight
And Prince Charming wakes me with a kiss.

Separate Ways

There was a road we travelled together.
Despite the differences we had seen,
There were spaces where we could meet –
Places that we thought would be for ever,
Till the hue of the moon turned green.

There were two paths where we parted,
Each with a separate journey ahead,
Both wishing the other could follow,
Wondering how this had all started,
Found its way to a marriage bed.

I left you neon signs brightly on,
Breadcrumbs like Hansel for you to follow,
But you were not looking for clues;
When I thought you were there you were gone
And I felt empty and hollow.

Contained in our world of screens and walls
We pretend not to see the divide –
You were off climbing ladders again.
Life is a series of curtain calls,
Behind which I was trying to hide.

Angry that you chose not to see
Patterns that we established long ago
Were limping on the stage of life;
These accumulated things absolved me
When the players left only the show.

Don't Ask Her to Talk About Love

Ask her to expand on theories of evolution,
She will talk on the pros and cons of revolution.
Discuss with the best about all the rest of the void,
Tell you news of some newly discovered asteroid,
But don't ask her to talk about love.

Ask her about the ocean, the sun, moon and stars -
Only her soul bears witness to the wounds and the scars,
And she knows lots about finding yourself and the soul's path,
Gladly tell about past lives if you promise not to laugh,
But don't ask her to talk about love.

She knows lots about astrology - don't mention trigonometry -
Will seriously speak of war zones at a push, even geometry,
Endless dialogue on the world and philosophy of life.
Her knowledge may surprise you, or cut you like a knife,
But don't ask her to talk about love.

And if you do ask her, the only thing you will hear
Is your own voice saying, "Hello! Are you still there?"

Leo

Be careful what you wish for,
For dreams can and will come true.
You are the Leo whose sun radiates
All the colours of my palette's hue.
You are my brother, my lover, my son,
Gift-wrapped with the blessing of One.
Leo activates my sense of humour, makes me laugh,
Came to help and guide me on the soul's path,
The Leo whose insight penetrates
All the emotions of my Gemini states.
With your gentle probing and silver tongue
You made communication into a beautiful song.
Your giving nature asks little in return
For my desire to grow and to learn,
And through the role of teacher
I will go where I am led.
Forsaking all my vows, my silent yearning
Brings strain to the marriage bed
For you have touched my soul with your mind
And the fire of desire is burning.

Like Doing Time: The Professor Speaks

There are similarities, you know,
Between the convict and the student:
Both are incarcerated, both doing time.
The Professor worked with prisoners long ago.

He observed them chalk upon the wall
(Time still left to serve before freedom),
Heard the students speak of school subjects
(Time left before completing them all).

Now, this was profound. I heard myself say,
"No more gazing out of the window,
Must pay your debt back to the system
Or you'll be back in school today."

It's hard to leave, almost habit-forming,
Killing time in this place we dream
Of what we would rather be doing
But submit to the power of conforming.

We must survive just a few more years –
Or could it be really for ever?
A future bleak, designed to keep us
Locked in progress, secure in our fears!

Stage of Life

We are all children floundering in the dark;
None of us are really in control here.
On the stage of life the curtain is up,
But there are no scripts.
The plots are hidden and the lines scrambled
So we have to fumble around trying to find them,
But mostly they elude us.
We do not understand.
We are pawns in a chess game,
But the game is life.
We can raise our hands to protect ourselves,
Hoping to divert the course of disaster.
We exert our will, knowing we are powerless
In the ultimate scheme of things.
We weave grand illusions and illusions of grandeur
Into the very fabric of our lives
In order to hide from our reality.
There is a small part to play here, we are sure,
If only we could discover what it is.
We are certain it would be purpose enough,
But we are all children floundering in the dark.

Knight in Shining Armour: Saved Again

So the age of chivalry is not dead!
As you came to bring us back to the fold,
Like two lost sheep you found us
Separated from our fallen gowns
And our loose morals.
You gathered us together as though we were jewels
Lost amongst some foreign field;
Restored us to our rightful places –
We women, soft and gentle, seeming often misguided,
Needing to be taken care of;
Too heavy a burden for ourselves
And others less qualified.
So you on your charger, gallant and merciless
In your protectionism, in full loving armour
Spoil all our possibilities.
With love and attention we are smothered,
Not knowing ourselves from children
Even though we are quite grown
And needing to open up and fly and make mistakes,
Take risks and teeter on the edge,
So that we know that we have been
And do not want to be rescued.

What Will It Take?

And so you love me, you say!
What will it take to show me?
Only from the ends of the earth
If I should need you to come,
Only this life and a past life
And an equation of any other sum.
Then once again in the lion's den
With your head upon a plate.
You would do all this for me?
And just because we couldn't wait!
What it would take to show me
Isn't something you could really see –
Illusion and reality are difficult for me.
As Thomas I am doubtful of motives
For love comes so easily.
Is this a well-constructed game plan,
Some universal rules devised by man?
It would take warrior or revolutionary
To break down all of my defences,
Unearthly harpist to resurrect my senses.
Love can't be measured by the spoken word,
Be the total of all we heard,
But it endures with a feeling,
On its own merit is spiritually reeling;
But I won't ask for very much,
Only everything to set my spirit free.
So don't you think that, like St Peter,
You would deny you ever knew me?

Verse and Worse

In the beginning there is desire,
Then the brain begins to malfunction.
You can feel your loins once again on fire,
Your head and your heart is without conjunction;
A battle rages to control your emotion.
Your head says suppression, time for work;
Heart says impression, wild love potion.
Give me enough rope, I may hang myself
Without even a push or a jerk,
Become a trophy on somebody's shelf.

Void

How can I think I know you
When a lifetime only tells me
What I did not know?
We see only what we want to see.
It makes us feel good
To think we have what we need;
But you saw through the void,
Reached deep into the heart,
Exposing the cracks and the flaws
Like you had been there before,
A frequent visitor,
Feeling all the vibrations.
Our two souls merged
And danced with an energy source
Made up of mind, body and soul.

Exposed

She is exposed and vulnerable,
Giving you certain advantages
In the way she displays.
Like the fixed gaze of a serpent
Ready to take its prey,
She knows the next move is not hers;
She will just lay down her claim
To self-control and surrender
For she has allowed herself to be seen.

Famine

As I lie in my sterile bed
I know you have stopped desiring me.
Was a lifetime too much to ask?
Did passion need to be set free?
A sadness comes when I think of the waste,
Of the giving and loving we both should taste -
And our paths are growing wider.
Separate and divided they are now.
How can I bring them back?
Why can I never show you how?
When did it happen? What was the time?
Where did it all stop beginning to rhyme?
We can agonize for ever and still not know,
But one thing is certain: we have ceased to grow.

Love Defined

Love is powerful,
Love is emotion,
Love is instinct.
Love requires definition,
But we never find it;
When we think we have it,
It changes shape on us,
Becomes distorted,
Out of proportion.
Love is obsessive,
Love is compulsive,
Love is habitual,
Love is not what it seems,
Love is in our dreams.
Love makes false promises.
Love is wolf in sheep's clothing,
Love is sheep in wolf's clothing.
Love cannot be trusted.
Love serves no purpose
Save that of procreation
For love is exclusive.
If I love you,
I hurt another;
Love is pain.
It is never pure.
Love is divisive.
It has limits;

Love is while it lasts.
It is what you feel.
Love binds and joins us;
It also separates us.
Love is what we mean at the time.
Love is for now –
Tomorrow our love will be different,
It will take on new meaning,
Look and feel different.
Love has boundaries.
Love is reactive.
Love is blind.

The Great Divide

And so this is how it is – she thinks
Everything is really fine.
It's as close as you get to baring souls
In this world that is not quite divine;
But she is content with the closeness,
With the way that it feels
As he gives her his time and his love.
There are no hidden agendas or deals.
She is happy that feeling has returned,
And shudders at her doubts.
Did she not know life was swings and roundabouts?
'It's here,' she thought. 'It is back again' –
Love to hold in her hand,
Something to share and something to stay,
Not something taken away, or given now and then.
She can fondle and grasp it,
Cradle and nurse it just as a lamb,
Nurture it with spiritual feeling
As deep as the ocean,
As simple as poetry of Omar Khayyám.
Kindled with fire and beauty and culture,
She will lavish her surreal sense of love.
Although just a man with a higher nature,
She will believe it is a gift from above.
He will see that he has worked his magic,

And then will suddenly retreat
Into his world of men's dreams,
Of competition, of winning and losing,
Newspapers full of big business schemes,
Of chasing balls around some field,
And for that game almost all will yield.
After all, what divides us
Is only a major tunnel vision –
Nothing more than the pursuits of opposites.
And if we somehow don't talk about it,
There won't be a collision or division.
But standing in the cold morning rain
As she surveys the harsh light of day
She knows how it feels again
To be like a twig blown by every current,
And know what she really held in her hand
Was just a grain of corn
From a good week's harvest –
Nothing more solid than an ice cube
Returning again to water at best.
That love is not immortal.

The Beauty of Thighs

I was sleeping;
Now I am alive again.
Poems flow freely from me.

You were dreaming,
Just living now and then.
It seemed to set you free.

When our paths crossed
The time was right,
But we could have closed our eyes.

For we weren't even lost
And we can't blame the night
For discovering the beauty of thighs.

Words You Want to Hear

Words can be manipulated.
If you use them, they become dull,
Usurped without definition.
They may appear to miss the point.
They become abused by common usage
As a whole nation adopts them –
Meaning is reduced to suit their purpose.
Words become oddities of shape and form,
Out of proportion, slightly deformed,
Unable to express themselves adequately
And part of a meaningless world.

Truth

This is my truth,
My perception of it
Which changes often
But is no less real,
Just as the wind –
Here today and gone tomorrow.

The strength and force of it
Is no less fierce in conviction
Than torrent or major hurricane.
It can't be bent or twisted into shape,
But remains steadfast,
As constant as the ebb and flow of tide.
It may go away,
But returns in full force
Once you have your back turned.

My Fortieth Year

In my fortieth year
It all began to seem clear.
I was at peace with myself
And had mastered the fear.

Secure in my body,
Understanding my mind,
I had learned that in love
The best was truly blind.

Love did not dictate
What could or couldn't be;
It had a life of its own –
A place for us to be.

Perhaps it was we willed it,
Created it out of need;
Fantasy or reality,
It sprang from the same seed.

It takes courage and insight
The gift of love to give.
That we have more than enough to share
He will understand and forgive.

Behind Closed Doors

She is running in deep water,
Holding tightly in control.
She doesn't know where her feelings are –
They have lost touch with her soul.

If she looks, she might see a wound
Almost as big as the world.
She crouches in her shell for protection,
Afraid to be unfurled.

But if you open the floodgates,
The prisoner might come out
To shed more tears – an endless river
Disturbed by chaos she sees about.

The imbalance of disharmony twisted her delight,
So she won't think and she won't feel
Or question what reality may reveal
But go about her business and conceal.

How Is It?

How is it
That we give our love
To those who cannot use it?
How is it
That we put our trust
In those who would abuse it?
How is it
That such meaningful words
Should fall upon deaf ears?
How is it
That such profound feelings
Lose themselves in tears?
How is it
That we're unable to reach
Soul to make us whole?
How is it
That recognizing the truth
Prevents a more noble goal?
How is it
That our lives unfold
Like a puzzle without any plan?
How is it
That some conquer the world
While others simple woman, or man?
How is it
That we are forbidden
The best fruit ever tasted?
How is it
The things we threw away
We should have kept, but wasted?

Old and Rusty

These words have lain in a drawer
To get old and rusty.
What is more,
These pages have bared their soul like you,
All wanton and lusty,
But I know not how to come out of the darkness,
Peel back the layers of my soul for you.
It is here that I am imprisoned by your beauty,
By a love that is steadfast and true,
So blow the cobwebs from these pages,
Spread a rug like Fatima by the fire
As we go down through the ages,
Taking our love ever higher and higher.

Images of Love: Passion's Song

Like a pebble, still by the ocean,
I lie there consumed with longing
To feel the full force of the water's edge
Take me by surprise with its swell
Then toss me and turn me over at will –
Waves at play with their hearts' desire,
Getting lost in the froth and dizzy with
Consummation.

I wait for the moment, parched from the sun;
Wait for the scent of perfumed sea spray
To signal approach.
Like seabirds swooning over the ocean,
Intent on the harvest of the soul's delight,
Wearing masks of pretence and disguise,
I show myself as an offering and surrender;
But they do not see me, lightly brushing over me,
Like the close encounter of a stranger's foot
Wandering lost in the moment,
Almost connecting.

I watch for the moon coming up
To show the colours deep within,
Wait for a hand to stroke my smoothness,
Raise the life force between thumb and finger,
Set me free upon the ocean's ebb and flow.
I mellow there in the darkness
Beneath the wet blanket of my desire.

Like Helloise praying for release,
I am slow to conquer my illusions.
I drink of the fountain,
Of all the forbidden fruits
That nourish and comfort me there;
I am stilled by the calmness of motion
As swell engineers a gentle release.

Once again I am buffeted,
Spewed out from the bowels of some great mouth
On to a vast, wide, sandy beach,
Cooled and refreshed by lips parting in the night.
I lie there uncovered and exposed by the light,
Already feeling chilled by the separation,
Until the light touch of a fresh wind

Stirs beneath my stony grave
And motions me towards the energy source.
Rolling and tumbling and gently rocking to and fro,
I am sucked into the timelessness of ages;
As the sand peels back its layers
I am dressed and undressed again and again
As passion gathers its momentum.

Oh, Yes

Oh, yes, there is some hunger
Immediately after the feast,
Where in some other space
You feel disjointed and unfamiliar.

Oh, yes, there is some hunger
After the long hello of expectation.
The closeness of arms and bodies
Is sometimes what you will miss.

Oh, yes, there is some hunger
In that very long famine
Of only a week or so,
But a strong impulse to go.

I Have an Ocean to Be Rid Of

I have an ocean to be rid of,
So I am here and not here;
You can't find me any place
Except the dark, deep blackness –
The depth of soul's despair –
Somewhere in the outer atmosphere.

I am floating alone,
Flying over rooftops and trees.
Space is all. I am detached
From all things, except the ocean
That has been my home,
Above and below the murky seas.

With eyes that fill like canyons deep,
Overflowing for ever
She passes through courtyards of history,
Trespassing in the graveyards of life,
Where headstones make you quiver
And angels don't deliver.

Where the heart breaks
And the river flows
Without plugs, she is unstoppable.
The breast of mountains heave.
No one can cross or enter
Where she alone goes.

I have an ocean to be rid of,
Visiting uncomfortable places
Where tears are honoured
Like a sacred port of call;
But if you discover these emotions,
She will eliminate all traces.

Choices

You live one life,
I live another.
Only in our private place
Can we be together.
The walls are lonely
Because no one sees us;
It's quiet sometimes
Because no one hears us.
But the dance goes on
And plays itself out,
For these are the roles
That we have chosen –
What other reason could there be?

Our Space

Only in our space
Can we ever be,
Just you and I
And all that would be free.

In another world
Where together we lie
With music that she has
Beneath our plaster sky,
Spreading rugs like Shiraz;

We question what is hard to know,
Speak of nothing small.
While the bonds of love grow,
Into each other's arms we fall.

Call it fate or destiny –
Perhaps all of this
When it is without reason
But too beautiful to miss,
And hard to leave in any season.

Blind to our difference,
Drawn only by how we are alike,
All pale into insignificance
When feelings of passion strike.

And who knows why,
As many have pondered before,
The fruits are given then taken away.
Like the tidal wave on the seashore
They cannot for ever stay.

So this moment in our hearts will last
Because it is timeless and for ever.
What is now may become the past,
But love we will not ever sever.

Sweet Seventeen

She's locked all her doors and windows
And refuses to feel,
Pulled down the shutters of her mind.
The rest she intends to conceal.

She must go fast and try to hide,
For life is short. She thinks
That the faster she goes
Might disguise her wounded pride,
But it is little yet she knows.

That it follows, like dowager's hump
Our baggage never far behind.
Like lost sheep awaiting collection,
Eyes are open but still are blind.

She will not speak of her woes
That simmer beneath the surface.
Sometimes she is angry, sometimes sad,
Insists that's how the story goes,
Maybe a little crazy or bad.

At times when friends may let her down
Of boys she will despair.
It's easy to block it all out,
But you know your mother will care.

But she's too proud to ask some help
Even when she may need it;
But it's good to see another side –
Together we might make pieces fit.

And Mother will try to be somehow better
At hearing when she talks,
So that mountains do not form
And become impassable where she walks.

So that her happy self can emerge
Once again into the light,
Be rid of the demons that come
And seem to want to pick a fight.

Invisible Again

She stands guard –
The keeper of the empty castle
Looking out on to a void.
Inside, vacant walls speak,
Look back at her,
Register her pain,
Become the vibrations.
These little actions
That she does from time to time
Secure her, imprison her.
A bit of giving here and there
Reserves her space.
She is motionless, transfixed,
Unable to move forward, or back.
She sees clearly what she has become –
Invisible again –
That she has allowed it
And dared to understand
That in her loneliness
She only wanted to be a part
Of the human race.
She was there for everybody,
But who was there for her?
Though she looked hard,
Didn't connect, reach, find, or touch
Where it mattered most.
She could be seen

Though she felt transparent,
Dangling herself obviously
In front of their attention.
Invisible to insensitive eyes
She awaits the return of her jailers,
Reflects that she made this her life –
The keeper of the castle.
She could choose to vacate,
Were it not altogether too risky,
For who knows what torment awaits
The bird with broken wings
That has not feathers enough to fly
When given the choice?
And so instead she quietly, patiently,
Waits for mood to pass
When courage fails her.
He waits only for her safe return,
From where she heals herself again.

I Lost a Friend Today

I should have felt better
But I didn't;
I lost a friend
And the world seemed cold,
More lonely,
But wasn't that what I wanted?

Unfortunately
The dog wagged its tail,
Couldn't work out
Why things were different.
Dumb dog, happy dog!
But my cat knew –
Instantly, instinctively –
That something was wrong.

I tried to explain,
But you know it's all bull to me.
However you look at it,
It could never be right,
It could never be wrong.
There were tears to my surprise,
Too many emotions to put in a song.

But I tried to remain calm.
It was what I had to do, you see.
I mean, there was no warning,
No dreams, or voices in the night,
Just a kind of knowing
That I had to make it right.

The pieces didn't fit.
There were no deep thoughts,
Just the plain, hard facts
In the cold, harsh night.
Reason was lost
In the senseless voice of time,
And nothing important came to me –
I couldn't make anything rhyme.

To push it all away,
To wipe the slate clean –
Wasn't that the intention?
To free myself from where I had been
And make myself invisibly seen;
To paint a work of art a bit,
Use all that wasted talent,
But it's all just bull and . . .

Time now to go with the flow –
I'll grit my teeth, you know,
Take it like a man,
Somewhat absent and impartial
As though I did not really care
To know the truth:
I lost a friend today.

No Illusions

Oh, yes,
Life is so beautiful
When it masks the ugliness beneath.

Oh, yes,
It is so perfect,
Covered by the rich cloak of promise
That tempts and taunts us
Like some wily whore
Beguiling with her powers.

Oh, yes,
I have seen your many faces,
Your colours rich with deception
Spread in order to dazzle,
To conceal what lies beneath
Are really maggots rotting.

Oh, yes,
Below the surface
All manner of things are lost
And lie there wounded and hurting
Abandoned by all notions
Of something better.

Oh, yes,
Those dusty maggots
Were always there
Should you choose to find them.
They will eat you alive
In your despair.
If you should choose
Not to be blinded with light,
There in the darkness
Is someone's reality.

Confused Mutt

I am dog,
Big-jawed, all male;
I lie down when I want up
To run in the field all day long,
But my fun is often curtailed.

In my dreams I roam and scavenge –
There are no restraints of leash.
I pee right here, I hump, I beg,
I'm allowed to hold on to your leg.

I put my nose to the ground –
Tracks can lead to anywhere –
And I am free to chase squirrels,
Feeling the wind in my hair.
That's how it used to be
For thoroughbreds, or mutts like me.

Before the scoop and doggie bag
And other social graces,
Before you went and had me fixed
So not to confront angry faces.

Before the Net or astronomical vet
There was a regular four-legged friend.
Find me a feast fit for a pet
And I promise to try to pretend.

We were hunters and retrievers –
Dogs with a day's work to do.
Now it's jogging round the block
Before you go and leave us,
Then complain how fat we grow.

I am dog,
Bored and displaced.
This doesn't quite work, you see.
Somewhat confused, often disgraced,
I am only trying to be me.

You see, an owl's gotta owl
And a mutt's gotta be a mutt,
So if I feel it's unnatural,
Pay me no mind when I ask you,
Do you think I am in a rut?

Melancholy

Melancholy fits like a skin.
After a lifetime of knowing you,
There is acceptance.

For whatever reason,
My soul is your comfort.
You reign there supremely, quietly,
Will not be displaced
By my dance of life
Lived in extremes.

I cannot shake your clutches;
No pleasures set aside your hold.
What dark secrets do you know
That bind us together?
What burdens of sins past
Do I carry for the world?

For I am the vessel
Of your Gemini suns;
You show me beauty in all things,
And, in all things, its opposite.
Somewhere the jester is smiling,
Mischievously spreading duality,
Poking fun at misfortune.
He sits on my shoulder,
As surely do the angels,
Tormenting, confusing, distorting
The vision of life's fabric.
Seen through gauze we find
Little glimpses of brilliance
Blur and fade sometimes,
Obscuring the clarity.

I make my peace,
Coincide and cohabit,
Embracing the elements.
I accept what is
And weep for what is not.

But I am still the warrior,
Still the pacifist.
Rebellious child won't rest
In the face of oppression,
The injustice of suffering;
For I have seen your many faces,
Know you intimately.
It is for you that my soul cries.

The Great Wall of China

I sometimes see us
Like the Great Wall of China,
Standing tall in a crusade
Of solidarity.

When we have troubles
No one is there for us.
In strength we will be perceived
As charity.

Together but alone
We keep the structure erect,
Like soldiers trying to protect
Ourselves.

From those who suspect
What we have is worth having
And will storm the walls, until
It falls.

The Illness

We cannot tell you, Mother,
What Tom and Harry said to Dick.
We cannot tell you, Mother,
Because you are so sick.
But who to tell our tales of woe?
Who will help us grieve and grow?
Where shall we find another brick?

In our solitude to ourselves we confine;
All of our hurt we must contain.
Each in our corner draw a distant line;
Each to his own to cope with his pain.
In a vacuum we try to comprehend
What only love alone can transcend,
If we could only get it back again.

We grow so old, yet stay so young,
Like children that once we were,
A family of dynamics far-flung.
But now we need our mother's fur,
Just as a dog will come to settle
On the warmest toes to test our mettle,
But we can no longer find her.

Lost and awfully wounded inside,
We recoil like wound-up springs.
Into our vacuum-packed shells we hide
From all of those unforgettable things
That perpetuate our silent days,
Destroy our love in so many ways.
Our guardian angel has lost its wings.

In the Hospital

Mother, I can't help you now
That you're on all this medication.
I don't know how to stop it –
This needle and pill dedication.
Once they get you hooked into the system,
It's all downhill.

Mother, I'm feeling helpless.
I can't even suggest what to take.
Once you lose the control of knowing,
It seems like you're just another mistake –
But not a mistake of nature,
That's for sure.

Mother, I lost you to hospital care.
Individual responsibility was too much for you,
Never knowing who or what to trust,
Whether to eat this or that and was it true
What some people said, while others differed?
It was too confusing.

Mother, I can't stop the roundabout
Where the inevitable is linked to intuition.
We can't see far down the road
When there is only a brief intermission;
But I am sorry to say goodbye this way
To one I love.

Guilty Bystander

In Yorkshire we are all one family here;
We talk out loud 'cause we've nowt to hide
And our lives revolve around beer.
It's "Hello, luv" as they board the bus,
And "Ta, duck" and "How ya doin'?"
All can be heard above the din
Of the ten conversations brewin'.

There's noise and clatter and gossip around
From one end of bus to t'other
As life is passed on in a hubbub of sound
To each person, the world, our sister and brother.
And if you think it, you say it to anyone near.
They care about each other's lives –
Might even share each other's wives!

And it's small and crowded and each day the same
Where the sky just lies there hovering grey,
But they've smiling faces even through rain.
They don't seem to notice with so much to say,
And it's "See ya" and "What ya drinkin', luv?"
"Goin down to t'corner shop, OK?"
They're busy doing nothing today.

Yet their world is so large!
How can I intrude or profess to say
Whether butter is better than marge?
That it's different 'tis true. Nowhere else
Would you find camaraderie like it,
But it isn't for all if you don't hear the call –
Some must simply luv it and leave it.

Yes, Mother

Yes, Mother, I am angry that you left us to fight amongst each other when you got sick.

Yes, Mother, I am angry that you were not there for me to link my arm in companionship.

Yes, Mother, I am angry that all summer you were coming, but just couldn't come, you said.

Yes, Mother, I am angry that your three children fell apart and broke away around your sickbed.

Yes, Mother, I am angry that all the things that should have happened in 1998 happened a different way instead.

Yes, Mother, I am angry that I have to be here instead of inside of my head.

Yes, Mother, I am angry that we all love you, and seems to be perfectly clear.

Yes, Mother, I am angry that without you nothing seems to work, and we are all acting very queer.

Yes, Mother, I am angry that your sickness makes you want to disappear and hide.

Yes, Mother, I am angry that you are afraid for us to see you like this, and we can't be by your side.

Yes, Mother, I am angry at you for causing such a commotion.

Yes, Mother, I am angry that we are possessive and selfish with our devotion.

Yes, Mother, I am angry that at this time I can't be more profound.

Yes, Mother, I am angry that we can't find any when faith and beliefs abound.

Yes, Mother, I am angry that we are uncomfortable about it and almost in a trance.

Yes, Mother, I am angry that my children will feel estranged from what should be a normal part of existence.

Hospital Beds

There must be better ways
To share a loved one's pain,
With a dignified end to our days –
Better than morphine's limited power
And monitored tubes, like entrails,
Hour after hour.

It is easy to envisage softness of sight and sound,
The comforting smells of lavender and cinnamon,
Fresh flowers, the colours of life around,
Gentle placing of cushions to dream
So their feet are close to the ground,
And harp and flute shall play away
In a room where love can be found.

Better this than the stark smell of medication,
Than the blue film of swollen veins
We have rubbed with our dedication;
Better a story to soothe our soul
Upon the smoke of heroin
Than a few choice words from a doctor playing God,
But still can't make us whole.

There is a case for euthanasia, every suffering person knows
With compassion a life we will to end
As our understanding grows.
A dog or cat we put to sleep –
A life with less severe incline.
It is because we love you
That you cannot take mine!

The year 2000 is coming, and we don't know who to trust,
But we must watch you suffer in pain.
As the dear God says we must,
So we do as we are told and take another pill.
When there is no improvement made
We find an anger left within us still.

To whom do we turn for comfort now
With shaken faith and belief?
No one can show us where or how
And when we finally submit.
Powerless to change it all,
We know that something didn't fit.

The Degree

It gets harder to stay focused.
Today there was an earthquake,
War broke out in a Third World
Where people only have one world.
I try to imagine for a moment, then
Bring the chaos happening all around me,
Back to my safe, warm, cosy settee,
Back to the reading for my degree.

Does it matter, I wonder, this theory,
The purpose of all I am learning,
When the harsh world comes knocking?
Yesterday rape, murder, more disaster.
I turn off the news broadcaster,
But still see all, hear all, know all.
Feeling small I take back control –
Time is elusive to meet my goal.

Body Image

Women's socialization begins at birth
With descriptions of soft, cute in pink
And our body size and shape determine our worth –
More important than what we may think.

There are cultural norms by which we conform
To prevailing ideals that say women are thin.
While purging and weight control become the norm
We try starving ourselves in order to win.

Body image results in babies too small –
No positive image here, just pregnant and fat.
Women don't seem to like their bodies at all –
Well, there is not much wonder in that!

To be young, thin, light-skinned and beautiful
Is what the popular media messages stress,
But this is only one step worse than dutiful,
And it's impossible to measure up, confess!

To adolescents media images cause harm;
Stigmatization of stereotypes prevail.
By casting judgment we sound the alarm –
It seems we set them up to fail.

Across all racial barriers and class divide,
Obsession with body image we find.
Fat causes an economic, psychological and social tide
Whose sanctions are very difficult to hide.

Anorexia and bulimia eating disorders
Result from prevailing social values.
There are no boundaries or cultural borders;
Women die to be thin on the billboard news.

When attractiveness determines body shape,
Women are objects of the media again,
Vulnerable to acts of violence or rape.
Less human, we can forget their pain.

But change is constant, that much is known.
Body image is not written in stone;
It has many factors of social interaction grown,
So we can change our body image to our own!

Buyer Beware the King-Size Bed

Buyer beware the king-size bed.
Take heed from one not newly wed:
The best of love is in your head.
Don't be fooled thinking bigger is better;
There's more passion in a small love letter,
For a love likes warmth and closeness,
No space to consider its grossness.
Though it looks good on Cinema 3
Space in bed to be artistically free
Can be the death of love, believe me.
In all that space you will desire sleep,
That mountain of room wish to keep.
Guarding it jealously you'll see it grow,
The space between you will begin to show.
You'll get your bed with lots of room –
From here it's kind of doom and gloom.
Where before you held her pretty face,
Now she longs only to keep her space,
For, once discovered, space becomes a habit.
Beware if you have ideas like the rabbit,
For there's nothing quite so complete
As to spread out from head to feet,
And once you discover this delight
Any invasive touch becomes a fight.
Space is an island with nothing in between.
My advice:
Take the smallest bed you have ever seen!

Torn

Torn between two polarities
Secured in emotional bondage,
She turns tricks, turns inward,
Tired of the games.
She is ready to run
Far from the scene of the crime,
Far from the men in her life –
All men.

Her strength is herself –
She feels the power within,
Knows the flow of energy.
Its protection, its saving grace,
Is her only salvation,
Must be her sole reality.
She is the master of herself,
Master of her loins.
The only influence she dare accept
Is her own.

Aunt Mary

I remember many a Sunday
After church I would go
On several buses all the way
To see Aunt Mary, you know.
I can still feel the thrill
When I think of it now –
The ease with which I went.
There was always somewhere to go,
And then a happy time was spent.
She was always glad to see you;
You were always welcome there.
Perhaps you would go to the woods
To walk, or simply just to be,
And you would usually be asked to tea.
To reach the house
There was a hill to climb.
The anticipation of who would be there
Was a feeling quite sublime;
But it didn't really matter, you see,
Because whoever was there
They would welcome me
And I would stay and play
Or talk a while.
We'd never fail to raise a smile
And bridge a gap or two.
Aunt Mary, I want you to know
I remember these things of you.

Feminist Counteraction

It is the children we must educate
About the dangers of bulimia,
Teach them before the age of eight
To think critically about the media.

Show them the ways they are deceived
Into believing that they are fat,
How all the media messages received
Translate into profit from this and that.

Expand their body-image notions
Of what beauty really could be,
Explore cultural roots versus beauty potions –
How empowering feelings can set you free.

Be a revolutionary, refuse to listen
To fat jokes wherever you find them,
And eradicating abuse can become the mission
You embrace like the national anthem.

Fight the economic and social sanctions
Imposed on fat women and men,
The discrimination faced in job-market action
Stigmatizes them all over again.

We must stop the fat prejudice
Of stereotypes by changing our ideas
Into positive ones, without injustice
Or any exclusionary fears.

Women become objects in that beauty magazine
Full of images that don't fit,
Existing in the fantasies of men's dream,
But we don't have to buy it!

Don't repeat bad media messages,
Counter argument with one of your own,
Insist on real body images
Where all sizes and shapes are shown.

Get over body size and move on,
Reject those products you see,
Resist until negative messages are gone,
Write letters and lobby for you and me.

Show positives to the sloppy and lazy,
Encourage with new ways to think.
Enhancing power is never crazy –
Try forging a feminist link.

A disparity exists between actual body size
And the cultural standard of women.
This is portrayed by media lies.
We must teach men that women are human.

By changing social culture from within,
Altering our own perceptions first,
By knowing we don't have to be thin
To achieve those dreams that we nursed.

Sexual Orientation

It's a minefield out there
For anyone of any sexual orientation.
Of these things we must be aware
Before we accept love's invitation.
We must learn to respect ourselves first
Then extend it to bisexual, lesbian and gay.
To be persecuted is the worst thing;
Respecting each other is the only way
To stop the oppression
And not be afraid to say
It's OK to be different today.

Homophobia

Do we need labels to define
The space we occupy together –
You in your corner, me in mine?
Can we never unite together?
Is difference a valid reason why
We can't love and respect
The identity of who we are
Without the need to defect?
Being different is not a reason
For the persecution of others,
For acts of violence or treason
Hurt our sisters and brothers.
Does sexual orientation define
The fear we hold inside
That he/she could be you –
The part we try to hide?

Peace-Organizing

With the goal of empowerment for all,
The women's peace movement is divided.
Themes of disunity runs throughout all;
The issues of strategy are undecided.

Feminists say the link to patriarchy
Is the gender trap to be avoided.
Protest on the basis of matriarchy
Cause harm and women to be exploited.

This gender system supports male violence
Within patriarchy, the family and state,
Links war and male power suffered in silence
To the dominant ideology feminists hate.

While peace and war are intertwined,
And the male monopoly of power alarms,
A battle of the sexes is what we find
Feminists advocate, taking up arms.

Undermining women's political power
Is the motherist focus, too narrow,
Emerging from an era of flower power,
The public arena from feminists borrow.

But the other side of the equation:
We look to the maternalist tradition.
They use motherist means of persuasion
To meet their goals, see them come to fruition.

It's where personal responsibility
Defines the action by the collective.
Social protest is within anyone's ability;
Their vision is a peaceful perspective.

The labels placed upon activism,
Whether feminist or motherist cause,
Actively working towards pacifism
Should be deserving of anyone's applause.

When the political becomes personal
Motherists are active in the community.
Their maternal baggage is a potent arsenal
Justifiably used with impunity.

Issues of women's values and sisterhood,
Bonds of friendship and sorrowful sharing
Lead to a feminist consciousness good
That's empowering simply by caring.

A World Not of My Choosing Today

I am wrapped securely in my cocoon.
No human intervention can find my spirit,
Or earthly encounter determine proximity,
For I am beside myself with despair.
I have no passion for a world I do not love.

I have cast the world aside assuredly
As it bears no traces that I wish to find.
Tomorrow will find me alive and perky,
But really I do not change my spots so easily –
I have never loved this world.
As God is my witness, time is hard to bear.

If you know me, find me with the underprivileged
At the door of injustice and betrayal –
Not in your group, or on your side,
But on the right side of standing alone
Because I have found nowhere else to stand.

For some of lighter soul than mine
This life is fun and folly and acceptance.
To me it's God's ridiculous joke played upon man
And seen by those less fortunate
To be the necessary evil to be endured.

Soul Music

When a woman cleans house,
Think of her not as ordinary
For no one is ordinary;
As she sets down her cloth
To wave her yellow duster
She becomes the gypsy in her soul –
As she spins around the kitchen floor
Happily entranced in music.

But do not catch her unawares.
This show is for her alone;
She has no need of audience
As she pulls forth this surge of life;
No need for applause,
As she writhes to the rhythm
Of her own music.

And do not think for one minute
That her talents have been wasted
As she performs gracefully
A ballet from the heart,
Or becomes a priestess in drag
Before a goddess moonwalk;
For she is transformed
And transforms all things ordinary
With her inner life
That only others find dull.

Sometimes

I am the anchor in your harbour.
Sometimes it's not enough
To be an anchor;
Sometimes I long for
Something larger.

These simple anchoring tasks
I chose myself –
Simple yet complicated,
By their grounding restrictions,
By the demands that they ask.

Sometimes I do not feel like an anchor,
But the anchored.
My free spirit weighted down,
Held by the burden of events,
No one remembers to thank her.

In choosing to serve she is humble;
Is choice ever really a choice?
Choosing between two evils
She builds on existing foundations
So the walls don't crumble.

Solitude

I have placed myself further
From the centre of all things,
Where I am here and not here.
On the fringes, in the wings,
My fragile existence is unclear.

I do not walk on the same path
As others that have gone before me.
Where I go, I go alone.
Body and soul shall disagree
To venture into the great unknown.

The Land

I thank God for the land,
For the healing powers found there
When the world is more than I can stand,
Grow courage out of despair.

When loss strikes at every chance
The buds of life are dressing;
The garden will still entrance
Even when sorrow is pressing.

The earth and sun are nectar to me
When seeds of life are wanting.
The sad soul dances with honeybee –
A life on the wing is hovering.

Small are the pleasures of grass and air
When first besieged by sorrow,
But large earth's comforts have some to spare
When faced with a bleak tomorrow.

Find growth and some rebirth
In land that lies fallow.
Find joy and a certain worth
In a heart that is hollow.

See beyond the land to church steeple.
There are mountains, hills to climb,
To people, missing people,
That can't be quenched by passing time.

But feel me here in this space
Where plant and tree do claim me
And burdens vanish without a trace
Beneath this crusted land set free.

Responsibility

To be alive,
To bear witness,
Is a burden great,
Like the first footprint
Left behind
Without a trace.
We each tread
Our own path,
Forging a reality
Uniquely our own.

Our Ancestral Home

In search of an ancestor,
Of ties that bind and separate,
Questions fester like a wound.
Was she kin? With whom did she mate?

This puzzle of branches lost
Descends bleakly into the unknown,
But he was more than John Doe, 1910-44.
There is a pattern here being shown.

It is impossible to trace
The soul of the human family tree,
For it becomes perfectly clear
That we are all one family.

The Old Mattress

This bed has travelled miles.
Where it goes, so do I.
There are layers attached to this bed
You cannot peel away
Without wanting to cry -
Layers you can only guess at.
But I will bring it suddenly close to you,
Into a new space, as a token of my love.
We will love it and mould it
And dress it all in blue.
After its rescue, we will withdraw
Silently and gently from it,
Till one day we will notice its miles,
See the grim stain of life.
When all of the pieces fit,
Like a true friend, we raise it up
And hold it dear until the very end.

Mother and Daughter

My daughter is getting married;
My mother is dying.
Even in the midst of life
There is decay;
In celebration
There is loss;
A sense of inner turmoil
Propels me to continue on
Into another day.
In a new space my daughter
Folds and sorts reassuringly,
A young woman's homeliness
Hiding the fear and uncertainty
Of the changes taking place
In her life, in my life.
Mixed emotions – joy and sadness,
Highs and lows – are shadows
Of her own inner turmoil.
Just as there is real growth,
There is recoil –
A dichotomy of opposites.
We laugh and cry then hug,
This strange process
Of change and growth,
Of rearranging
The habits of a lifetime
All submerged
Into the colour of a new rug.

These fun and brilliant new ideas
All walk about
On the surface of things –
Colour schemes, feng shui
And wedding rings.
Underneath lies many lifetimes
Of experience
Brought to the marriage bed.
For a moment our own intuition
Disturbs us,
Becomes a faint echo in our head;
The joy of new beginnings
Emerges through the window
As sunlight
Fills the newness of the house
With promise.
This on again, off again
Fight-or-flight of emotions
Is briefly quenched;
Soon it will all become familiar again
And she will look back
Only now and then.

Moving Day

I cried for the end of childhood
As I packed and sifted and sorted
Too long - a delayed reaction.
This was not to India, or China,
Just to a new neighbourhood;
Anywhere else would have been
Devastating.
Was it the emptiness of drawers,
Or childhood memories?
The thoughts I had of my own mother -
Leaving her for another country?
Was it the sudden quietness of the room,
The trials of youth echoing,
Or my own daughter's tears?
The bewilderment of dog and cat
Sitting in the space where she sat?
It all blurred to shake the emotions
And to heighten our fears,
Dislodge all that we had accumulated
Over the years -
The end of childhood's doings,
And innocence
Screaming from each suitcase.
The habits of twenty-three years
Not easily put aside
As you struggle to maintain sense.

Yes, this is leaving day,
Like emigration day all over again,
Like the hardest thing ever done,
Revisited.
For a moment it quells the young and spirited
This sudden emotion rises up,
Makes holes in our belly,
Washes over us and seems
Unstoppable.
There is nothing gradual about
This process;
It demands instant surgery –
The cutting-away, the letting-go.
No matter how angry at yourself,
The tears just flow.
After the first night she came home,
Homesick.
Yes, now I remember
So many vacations cut short,
The long telephone calls
From far-off places –
All the support I could lend her.
Packed now
And ready to grow!

Spencer: Four-Legged Friend

Born on the second day of September –
We will remember.
You came to us when we needed you.
We didn't know it, but we grew;
And everyone knew you, if not us,
Right down to the last child.
You honoured them with your love and trust.
They saw you as everyone must.
You were Spencer, Spence,
Bud or Buddy –
A character we loved
Even when muddy,
Who came to greet us with slipper or shoe,
A sock, some underwear.
Everyone knew.
You came to teach us
About what really mattered.
It was not the fur you left about,
But love that never shattered.
You came to make us laugh,
To show us how to play,
To enjoy a walk, a swim, a talk.
You taught us courage
And patience as you watched us
Every day.
We told you all the things
We had to tell
When no one else would listen.
You bore our burdens
And suffered bravely,
Even though your silence
Was sometimes deafening.

You taught us well;
We loved you well.
Born in September –
The winter will be a time of you,
Rolling in the last patch of snow
Of being kind to cats,
Sharing your bed and water with Miranda,
And never quite catching the squirrel
But enjoying the chase;
Of long grass and meadow walks in fall,
Of Bruce's Mill, your favourite place of all;
Your grin from ear to ear,
Your love of water,
Swimming out without fear
And jumping off docks,
And fetching balls
But never bringing back,
And Dogeden and Jen,
And Halloween again
When all the children come to see you;
Of food, yours as well as mine,
The delight of Spencer's life –
Fooood, so divine! –
And words you hated to hear:
"No garbage, Spencer!"
Was never that clear
And "No more!", "Had enough!"
How could enough ever be enough?
And the park belonged to you –
It was where you played and grew.
Your friends were there,
You marked your spot –
There was Rocky, Honey,
Benny, Hershey – the lot.

You ran freely possessed
With the youth of years
That no one guessed,
Always so fit and so full of life
In between a pause and moment of rest.
You were the teacher even of dogs –
No malice or spite,
Just a gentleness of light.
You lay in submission
And allowed the way
To freely unfold
With each new day.
Your large frame and paws,
Your head with a bump
And your comical smiling jaws,
Your eyes brown and kind
Accepting it all.
Whatever came,
You answered the call.
You were haughty
And you were proud
And only sometimes naughty,
And quite magnificent
In your earthly shroud,
Princely and strong,
A lion gone wrong,
A teddy bear large
And cuddly and long.
We could stroke and squeeze
And would sit by his side,
Then would give you a paw –
Ready for a walk?
He could spell with his jaw.

Through the ravine and the woods
To the end, or the park
On our usual walk,
He would rarely bark
Save stranger at the door;
But at Dogeden it was different –
He was the ringleader there
So he barked more.
And Pet Smart knew him –
His very own store.
It was here he got treats
And they gave him more.

We lost him early – too soon –
And we never knew
How sick he really was.
It was so very quick.
He was silent and brave,
With no noise of suffering.
He taught us to laugh,
To relish life and to love it
Even to the grave.
He was our dearest friend
And we loved him too well.
Of his praises
There is too much to tell.
He taught us to fetch the ball,
To follow as well as lead,
To relax and let life flow.
Love was his creed.
So we salute you, Spencer,
And let you go
Where all the best dogs go:
To the happy hunting ground

Where doggie friends are found,
Green pastures all day long to roam,
Even love with a pretty hound
And doggie dreams all day,
Rolling in the snow,
Leaving his mark too many times
In places where love will grow,
And a bone after lunch,
And then brunch and munch
As much food as he wants,
Where no one cares if he gets fat,
And no one moans or grunts,
And he can swim all day in the lake,
And then come home to tea,
And he can abide in love,
And can at last be free
To be like a doggie should be.
And we will love him for ever
And hold him dear.
In our hearts we remember the joy
That he brought to our lives.
So from now until then
Be a very good boy
Until we meet you one day again.

Home

My home is my sanctuary,
The mother of my womb.
It is my refuge
And my retreat,
Where I regroup and
Recoil from defeat.
My home is also my prison
And my tomb,
Protecting me,
Loving me.
It will not set me free.

The Operation

At eighty-two we put our trust in God
And the surgeon's hand.
We must forgive ourselves
For thinking that a common rod
Is not a magic wand.

Let us try without anger to pretend
That the operation signed for
Was a new lease of life to mend,
Not to leave her there at death's door.

They sliced her open with a knife,
Took a kindly look inside
At the short, thin veins of her life
That flowed with the trust of ages.

With all the new technology,
The intelligence of sages,
Surgeons decided without apology
To abort, and sewed her back up again.

For we are surgeons, powerful are we,
Meant to save the lives
Of eighty-two-year-olds who put their trust
In God and mistakes of surgeons' knives.

Wake up thinking all is just grand,
Proud we made the journey –
So we shake the surgeon's hand
Without the power of attorney.

Then tell her just because it's free
Suffering was all for nothing.
"Suffer little children to come unto me,"
Says God, and just because life sucks!

Injustice

The seat of my anger, my pain,
Lies deep in the small of my belly
Where great weeping, heaving, begin –
Hide the violent scream within.

There is no door or window here.
The floodgates are held in check
Like stones rolled against His tomb.
For anything else there is no room.

Pain gathers and hides in sorry places
Deep in old wounds still festering,
Like birds resting on high wire
She fights for control of inner fire.

Anger at wrong choices made,
At blunders of man inflicted upon man,
Visited and revisited once again.
Ask why – is just because they can.

Yet needing to win sometimes
While recounting life's losses –
Breath held in against its will
Is released to fall as earthly crosses.

All Kinds of Love

Love that binds us tight
As noose around the neck
With love that is kind and giving,
Is bent on self-sacrifice,
Has little to do with living.

Love does not reach or grow
In places where it should,
But maintains its imperfections
Knowing they are in full view,
Shielding, protecting the reflections.

Love in all its absurdity
Rejects all other possibilities
To expand without consideration.
It holds you in high esteem
Against possible inflation.

Love that has a silent jailer
Makes a prisoner of itself
Because it cannot leave
What holds it strong, or
Be happy while others grieve.

Love that is blinded by itself,
Is oblivious, does not consider
Consequences for the other.
The moth is protected by the jar, but
Self-sacrificing love can smother.

Love that is hopelessly enduring
Feeds upon itself
Becomes self-contained.
Enclosed in its familiar actions,
Its worth is maintained.

All kinds of love exist,
Bound by secret, ancient codes
Based on the strangest notions.
We try to live our lives
In accordance with love's emotions.

Love that is all things
Can be debilitating,
Stifling in its obsessive care.
It is both selfish and selfless –
Beneath that, another layer.

Who so is conjoined together
By God or other quirk of fate
Is not easily put asunder;
If pain is the price of gain,
Can there be rain without thunder?

Living in our truth
Of love that binds and ties
Both here and on the other side,
We freely choose our way
And decide what will abide.

The Circle of 'When?'

I really don't think it's working,
Darling.
You are so busy perking
And business-ing your life away.
Do you know what I did today?
Or care to see me grow?
I punish you by eating food
To fill the empty spaces
That still refuse to show.
My cover to the anger of mood
Returns each time you go.
I live with you and yet without
A fork in the road of separate ways –
A silent road where inside I shout.
Tell me what this is all about?
Returning now to sleep off your hunting!
I am too tired to be really there,
Singing 'Bye, Baby Bunting',
Playing mother bear.
I lose you again and again
To crossword puzzle and pen.
I only meet you now and then
In the circle of 'When?'

Prayer

The earth moved on its axis today.
The sun revolved,
But I lost my way.
Help me, Lord,
For I am here and not here –
A prisoner of time
Through the ages, immobilized by fear.
I would serve something worthy,
Some cause or action found,
But I remain in my vacuum
Where useless gifts abound.

Cherokee Blood

You,
Part of my Cherokee blood,
What did I recognize
In your soul's eyes?
Was it the deep-brown
Hazel of the ages,
Or a kindred spirit
In a war that rages?
Sometime long ago
There was you and I
And the buffalo.
I took a spear into my side
In battle, and in anger died
From slow and hideous wound
That left its triangular mark
Just to remind me
That I can't see all things coming.
On the trail of tears walk –
I will find you again.

These Are Important Times

There is a war going on
Somewhere where women can't show skin,
Contrasting to the West,
Where little girls are made to look like grown-up dolls
And put in contests to win.
But we are fighting our own wars here,
Deep on the domestic front,
Where lack of time and solidarity with each other
Has become an affront to our senses.
Still we are offended when brother kills brother,
Never turning the other cheek,
And all in the name of Allah.
This solution to war we seek.
When God is on our side
How could we lose?
I ask you, how could God choose?
One life is not greater than another.
My East and Western friends,
You are my sons and daughters,
My husband, wife, sister and lover;
Many lives I have lived in your lands
And you in mine;
I have been Jew in Jerusalem
And Arab in Palestine;
I have natively roamed with the buffalo
And trapped my way over lands where beaver go;
I have taken part in your crusades, witch-hunts
And battles fought on many fronts.
Both East and West I have lived and seen –
There is no difference between.
The shades of love are not red, but green.

On Waking

It quickly passes through my head,
'Why there is no one in my bed?'
Is there supposed to be someone there?
I try hard to remember and declare,
"Oh, yes, you went away yesterday –
I am alone again."
What more is there to say?
I can't remember when
Or if I'm supposed to be alone,
Or if that's just the way I've grown.
It's like a dream when I'm awake
That I cannot seem to shake.
Is there supposed to be someone there
Lying close to me, touching my hair?
I can't remember any more.
Then I recall you on another shore,
Dividing your life here and there.
It's not my turn for the spare;
I can't find you anywhere.
You are busy wheeling and dealing.
I don't know what I am feeling –
I've grown accustomed to it all.
Between us there is a wall –
I can't remember why it's there
Or if there should be more to share.
I wake up one more night confused,
Alone. I feel a little used.
I can't remember when or where
We decided upon this meagre share.

When I wake up alone
I remember that seeds were sown,
And this is the way I've grown.
I can't remember when you were there last.
The pattern set in and the die was cast.
At the side of me there is a space,
But I can't make out a face.
Am I dreaming or awake?
This blurred line is no mistake.
Am I meant to be with you?
Shouldn't we be stuck like glue?
Why is there a place by me,
Empty for all to see?
I turn over and go back to sleep,
Remembering there is just me.

The Connection

I called you today.
I was beside myself with emotion –
The connection made me dizzy,
Made me dance in the love potion.
I couldn't concentrate on anything
After hearing your inflection.
Everything was light, symmetry and colour –
A canvas too perfect for inspection.
And it wasn't the things we said
Or forgot to say along the way,
But what we held in our hearts and heads
When we made the connection today.
We knew it was there to stay;
It was too difficult to contemplate
The excitement mixed with tearful elation,
The ins and outs and strangeness of fate
As familiar as a long-lost relation,
Connection comforting and spiritually clear.
You asked me not to disappear;
I promised that I would still be here.

Fading Beauty

It is harder to be beautiful now.
The sunset on the twilight of life
Takes longer to paint a palette of recognition;
Harder to make eyes dance like they used to
Dance, more like the woman feels inside,
Still vibrant, vivacious and alive.

Strange to see my reflection in the mirror
Staring back at me! I wonder who that is?
Not the head-turning woman that I know.
Tell me: where did the soft look go to?
She is wearing it, but it doesn't show.

It isn't that you mourn her death –
The passing is liberating in many ways.
A mask hides the child, the woman inside.
Mind plays tricks on what we see and feel –
Gaps between feelings and recognition wide.

Time has gone by and taken our youth,
And it surprised us with what was left behind.
It is still the same life, still the same wife
Who is fading into adversity
And a phase in life that isn't very kind.

But she still looks good as he does.
We forget women often look so much better;
And men never think that they might have changed.
Perceptions are where you cast your net.
In her circles she can still cause a buzz!

Why I Hate Christmas Now

Where expectations run so high
With promises that can't be met,
A let down for the Gemini
Is bad for the soul and mindset.

In the build-up people are crushed –
Sadness remembering times gone by.
Achieving such perfection is rushed,
And emotions are running sky-high.

People are lonely at Christmas,
From family and friends are separate.
For one day only make all this fuss –
What reason is there to celebrate?

Then why not celebrate every day?
Not highlighting who has more or less,
Separating and dividing in every way
And adding to the pain and stress.

How can I celebrate the torment you know,
Insisting we all have such fun?
If 'Frosty Snowman' plays again, I'll blow
Or will attack like Atilla the Hun.

When the tree and trimmings are up there,
Stressful moments of anticipation.
Of everyone's feelings we must be aware -
Will there be disappointment or elation?

But you can sense disaster brewing
In some unchecked spaces forgotten -
Panic attack, someone choked when chewing.
On this day someone is feeling rotten.

More buying and giving we really don't need,
I try not to make it too clear.
These commotions seem more like greed
To put us all in financial arrear.

In Case You Didn't Know

In times of crisis you were always there for me,
Standing shoulder to shoulder across the great divide.
I could always rely on you to show me the way I couldn't see.
You would still move heaven and earth to be by my side.

When we have a moment of nothing much to say,
You search for something more to fill that space
And I am aware and I care what you do with such grace –
Anything that it takes to stay in the winning race.

Our paths of separate ways tried to divide us for ever.
To be a part of my life you fought hard
And never missed a special moment in our life together
To record with some fine words written on a card.

Our deepest emotions they often went unsaid.
You were always thinking how to impress me next,
Never ceasing to surprise me with flowers or what was in your head –
So solid and grounded I would love you even when vexed.

My rock and my anchor in any port of call
We navigated a safe harbour and protective home,
And I want you to know now that I have no regrets at all;
I want you to know that I have no desire to roam.

You continue still to impress me with your constancy,
Steadfast like knight or warrior to the cause be free,
Bearing allegiance to family. On this solidarity I agree.
I love you for all this and know that you love me.

Christmas in Canada

You know I still get a thrill
Out of seeing different cultures.
Buy their cranberries at Christmas –
Their assimilation surprises me still.

Wishing each other the holiday best
Reminds me how we are all the same.
Once removed from our backgrounds
We are busy with this often adopted fest.

Right down to the turkey and stuffing –
No one will miss a bit of mistletoe or holly,
Not Chinese, Egyptian or Indian.
We are all brought together over plum pudding.

United in the land of Canada,
We fought so hard for these customs,
Travelled far to make them our own,
Transforming the world into wonder.

The Technological Age

A time to be young and free!
I thought I was doing too well –
All the changes bounced off me
In the sixties flower-power spell.

Then all began to disappear.
The things we took for granted –
Jobs, the way we lived our lives –
Became off-balance or slanted.

We were not old, and yet extinct,
Replaced like the dinosaur.
In thirty years so many changes –
Things we don't need any more.

First people went, then jobs went
Along with self-respect.
'Retrain' and 'rebirth' they said
Of those who would defect.

No chance to see what is coming,
Our choices were only to change,
But some got lost in the takeover
Outside the 'normal' range.

There were artists and shipbuilders –
Brush shipwrecked without a clue.
There were talents without a skill
Or knowing what else to do.

The strong did not help the weak
Find a place in this new world:
It was every man for himself
To see how the story unfurled.

But it's a race to the death
In the global economy.
Everything else is trivial -
Writing, or astronomy.

Now is the computer age,
But not everyone can find a place
To put their hearts into
Within the economic race.

There is nostalgia in old tricks -
Hard to lose paper and pen.
Coal miners no longer needed,
Back to old ways now and then.

But who can shut out the world?
So now I surf with the rest;
I am a mental traveller -
I scan the world from my desk.

When I look up from my window
And wonder from where I have come,
If this is the ultimate goal,
How come I still feel so dumb?

Rock and Anchor

I know my place:
I am the rock and the anchor.
My feet extend through the earth
Like tentacles
Clinging to life
For all they are worth.

I am swayed and shaken
By hurricane and earthquake;
I am pounded and impaled
Upon that rock
To which I am anchored.
All things frozen in time
Are now unveiled.

The rock and anchor that I am,
Part of the universe.
That which will be, will be
The law of the universe.
All is as it was meant -
The rock and the anchor,
Part of the fabric, part of the cement.

In my safe harbour
There is calm and peace;
Momentarily between the storm
I offer you safe passage through,
Only to meet again where tides foam
And spill and spew with shipwreck
Until we can all return home.

Inertia

Is this inertia
The quiet before the storm?
As I reside under bedcovers
I am aware this is not the norm.
Is this apathy?
Something that resonates
With impending doom?
This conserving of energy
Can't be swept away with a broom,
In this state of readiness
And unreadiness
Waiting like a cat for prey,
Quietly motionless.
What will be the test today?
Prepared for that which comes,
Waiting for the next blow to fall,
She sleeps to hear the drums,
Transfixed like the deer,
Sensing danger but not knowing
From where, or how, it will show itself.
But this knowing carries no fear;
It is ready to give of itself
Until all illusion passes
Into the sleep of those who know the truth.

Conflict

Palestine, your massacre
Heralds blood around the world
To fall on powerful hands
And not so powerful hands.

Politics, money and greed –
This is the only creed.
No longer can we pretend
To be blind, deaf and dumb.

I am sad for my Jerusalem –
It belongs to the centuries,
It belongs to us all;
I am neither Palestinian nor Jew.

But I see you clearly,
You who cried holocaust
And learned nothing from it.
The abused become the abusers.

Stealing land for profit –
Yes, like colonial powers did,
Yes, like the West settled
By spilling blood of Indians.

America, my heart cries for you.
Who have torn down your own towers
And led the world to chaos,
Left me with blood on my hands?

Palestine, I know you well;
Your brave struggle endures
The lack of humanity shown,
But mourning lives in the soul.

Still waiting for justice
Under Milosevic, I watched
Other massacres take place
In another time and space.

Who are these Caesars
Bent on destruction?
Call them by what name you will,
God's archives are full to overflowing.

One day we shall answer His call.

No Time Left

Oh, Mother, you crossed over when I was in Florida.
St Augustine was tugging my shoulder and knee.
I walked the treadmill and a hotel corridor
To be ready to greet twenty-five people with glee.
Getting ready, the phone seemed urgent to share
Its sad news and shockwaves, brother in tears –
Despair – despair because I wasn't there!
"Don't think I'll be able to do it," he said.
"Oh, yes, you will," I said, to calm his fears
Ten minutes before I greeted and ate.
I smiled and covered my inner emotions;
I died in my solar-plexus state.
The role I played covered my devotions.
I ate more than usual, gave toast to Millie,
But later that night the knots in my stomach
Brought the shivers and the endless chilly,
And the only good night's sleep that I had.
I dreamed, after eleven years, of Willie.
I woke up and cried, was angry at them all.
They didn't tell me that I ought to come –
I was still entertaining at the ball.
And I couldn't understand what Dad had meant,
Was angry at him and I cried for a while,
But like an angel for my mother he was sent.
And we told the children, then the party crowd.
With words and eye-watering condolences,
And flowers, but still no tears were allowed –
Just cold chills and the pits of stomach aches,
Like heartaches, solar-plexus stakes driven
Into churned-up wasteland of shivers and shakes.
It all seemed so surreal.

At home, unpacked, the next week was spacey –
The strangeness of distance and controlled thought.
I planned with my sister with heart still racy
A funeral that must be conceived and bought –
The flowers and phone calls, times and places.
We asked what she would like. We have to know
The words and music and social graces,
And it's one day up and the next day oh!
But today I seem strangely elated.
I have to get out or go into town,
Abandon all that I have equated –
Christmas shopping or a new ball gown.
And then Wednesday came, bringing Katie's dream,
Of Granny in sunshine with purple, yellow flowers,
Blue shorts and spotted swimsuit. It would seem
That she was spending many happy hours.
It was then that I knew she had crossed over.
This message was her way of telling me
She was running down the hill like Rover
And she had found a better place to be.
Then all week long I held a candle ritual,
Guiding her from Bardot towards the light.
It burned to light the way for Mildred Moores,
And I am certain that she won her fight.

Then I was packed again and on my way.
I did not love the grey northern sky,
But many a memory blew away
Before I had found the answer to 'Why?'
No sleep to be had in the hotel room!
It burned with fire in the middle of the night
And it swept us all out into more gloom,
Making front-page news in the morning light.
Was this trickery, or testing of us?
Were you causing this commotion, Millie?
And did you want to do it just because?
We were tired, but it went awfully chilly.

Mother

I didn't sleep, or dream of her at all.
I lay awake dismantling a life,
Seeing the pictures on the wall.

The house had always made me happy,
But after dismantling a lifetime
Our duty and efficiency was crappy.

Especially when I dared to find you
Saving blue shorts and your flowered shirt,
Nose pressed against the smell of cloth still new.

The toughness of any decision!
What we shall keep and what has to go
We separated with such precision.

You helped to guide us through this, Mother.
Your presence we felt was everywhere -
No cross word to sister or brother.

The small things that I needed to find -
The paper, the stone, the wood, the art -
To the rest I was somehow blind.

The library man came while we were there.
A coincidence? Not very likely!
You sent him to make us aware.

With incense cleansed each room for you, Mum,
So that you could be free of those rooms
In the way we had always done.

With you at the funeral parlour –
Even the florist came while we were there.
He was no unsuspecting caller.

The source of you saw us through it;
Your thoughtfulness made it easier for us,
Leaving behind no loose ends to fit.

Mother, you were so proud and so strong.
I wanted you to be heaven-bound –
I hope you are where you belong.

The Funeral: Everyone Cried but Me

I had to see it over,
I had to see it done,
I couldn't fall apart
In front of everyone.

When all around me cried
I knew that I was strong.
Do I know myself at all?
Is there something very wrong?

I heard words about being brave,
Talk of being very strong,
Wrote the words to be said
And even found the song.

I held a hand
And gave a smile,
I greeted then I hugged,
Even partied for a while.

I lit a candle –
The centre was Mum.
We worked the reception room –
Almost everyone could come.

Is this what I learned well
To cover my deepest emotions?
Even a distant acquaintance
Showed more of their devotions.

Or was it Mother that I knew?
You were free to be well.
Had I learned to let go –
To love you and say farewell?

You are in a better place –
Of that I have no fear.
And later in my private space
Miss you and hold you dear.

The Millie Star

I had to be strong, Mother.
I couldn't just break down.
Knowing we relied upon each other,
I couldn't wear a tearful frown.
They watched my face for signs.
There was nowhere to escape –
Love that ties and binds
Wears a strange mourning cape.

Everyone's eyes filled with tears.
Was I heartless to be brave?
I dried up my feelings, their fears,
I could not grieve upon your grave.
A life we celebrated to the end
Requires no sadness. Where you go
Can bear no tears where bodies mend.
This you will understand, I know.

So forgive me, Mother, if I seem too strong.
I do not know myself in my own power.
To whom or where does this powerful strength belong?
I am quick to anger, but strangely calm.
How can I grieve when I'm sure that I know
The place you are in is safe from any harm.
And I wasn't there when it was time to go,
But in Katie's dream you were safe and warm.

Oh, dear Mother, Mother, how can I know
If what I am feeling be right or wrong?
You will no longer be able to tell me so.
Can death as well as life make you be strong?
I busy myself, Mother, so as not to think
How vulnerable and fragile we all are.
If you are looking down, give me a wink,
And I will find you on the Millie star.

Mother, I Hope You Find Your Angel

Mother, I hope you find your angel
And you get your purple hair.
I hope you dance your socks off,
Round the moon without a care.

Mother, I hope you're eating chocolate
With old friends and family near,
Feeling good in your new body,
Even if it's only atmosphere!

Mother, are you planning your next trip
To earth or to beautiful chasms there?
Told your parents it's time to get a grip,
And you and Willie are having a sip.

Mother, I hope you are wearing red
And making your presence felt,
Knowing that you are God's child
Now you can make all hearts melt.

Mother, I hope you have made your case
For understanding and peace for all.
That will help the human race -
Know if God is on the ball.

Mother, I hope you're in the sun,
Swirling the bright colours around you,
Dazzled by the hues of every one
Now your eyes are good as new.

Mother, are your cares of the world gone?
Can you tell us what you find?
Is there a place for everyone
Or must we hope that God is blind?

Mother, what markets and clothes are there?
Are you wearing your three-inch heels again
Or glad no worries about your hair –
A proud Leo in a lion's den?

Mother, are you taking découpage?
Into books or cartoon-making?
Is heaven as consumed with large?
Are you on the Millie star baking?

Beauty: The Irony of It

All the loving, the preening,
The waxing, the creaming,
All the nail-polishing
And the hair-removing,
All of the hair-caring
And the eye-checking,
Doctor appointment,
Medical annointment,
Functions of life,
Curling of eyelashes –
All end up in a jar of ashes!

Miranda Died Today

If you were a cat in the wild,
You would find another way to die;
Send out the signal you were beat,
Ready yourself to be someone else's meat.

And this is the law of the jungle
All animals can understand,
But I must take you to die today
By the veterinarian's hand.

And you, my faithful little friend,
Who was always there for me,
After seventeen years of devotion
It's now the time to set you free.

In this un-catlike existence
You walked proud, protecting your ground,
And no greater guardian was there,
In man, or other faithful hound.

Never wandering far from home,
Gracious, ladylike in your ginger coat,
She and I into colour blending,
Was content upon others to dote.

A female, strong and tolerant
Seeking cold water from the tap,
Kraft cheese slices, fancy feast
Treats and a wish for a comfy lap.

She drove all other cats away.
Miranda didn't ask for more –
Even when the birds annoyed her
Would bring them sometimes to my door.

Intelligent there is no doubt,
What ancient pastures in your eyes
Brought your wisdom and knowing
To help us in our own growing?

We thank you for the gift you gave –
The closeness and bond that we shared.
Thank you for a job so well done,
And leave knowing that we all cared.

Cat

I shed my tears for you, my friend.
The house seems empty,
Without life,
Becomes mere shell,
Makes null and void everything
Without your presence.
Not even music can transcend
Your absence.

Full Circle

A new baby!
The celebration of life –
A life that insists on being born.
Rebirth of one waiting in the wings –
The circle of life again begins.

Mourning doves are back again
With spring,
Ready to begin to nest,
On my window sill to rest.

There is a wedding afoot –
The stirrings of new beginnings,
The warmth of summer trimmings,
Buds forming, winter leaving
Behind any grieving.
Life springs forth anew, undaunted.
In the wake of war
Sheer joy is flaunted.
The whole world wants peace –
Something to give thanks for.

Turning full circle,
No time to rest upon dissent.
The earth moves busily on its axis.
Nature will not repent,
Is loud and calling to us.
Life is good and full of promise.

Enjoy!

Citizen of the World

I have a haunting Celtic soul,
An Arab-eyed soul.
I have a Jewish music soul,
A grey-street English soul.
I have a bright-light Arizona soul,
An ancient-history Egyptian soul,
A mysterious Zen soul.
I have the thoughtful calm of aboriginal Indian soul,
The magic and excitement of gypsy soul.
I have a Canadian pioneering soul,
A monk's lonely soul.
I have a Russian artist's soul,
A Roman warrior soul.
I have the chic of a French temptress soul,
The adventuring of a Spanish seafaring soul.
I have the wild of the Rastafarian soul,
An age-old revolutionary soul,
The wisdom to know the forests soul.
I have the expansiveness of the Americas soul.
I am a citizen of the world.

Could It Be?

Our love has plateaued into coexistence
With polite and sometimes not so polite exchange,
Where excitement has been replaced by virtual resistance
And indifference likened to the Outer Hebrides range.

Where space and time fail to meet on any level
Our intentions are not confrontational,
But our minds wander in unused places, travel
To where they once were conversational.

Why do harbours and anchors still hold strong
To the wrecks to which they have become accustomed,
Cradling and festering their desire to belong
When all avenues have already succumbed?

To possible reflections of seeds not sown,
Of dreams with bilious anticipation,
Could it be a monotonous tone
We try for lack of validation?

The Absence: Goodbye, Mother

When I awoke it was there,
That feeling,
Like something was missing –
Something not quite right in the world.

When I surfaced each day,
A sense of absence,
A gap that could not be filled,
An ache that would not go away.

I awoke knowing something was wrong,
Unable to put my finger on it.
For a moment I floundered
Without anything to hold on to.

It was nothing concrete,
Nothing I could easily explain,
But something didn't make sense
Because you were no longer in my world.

Your absence was acute,
I felt the void all around me.
Nothing could change it.
Where you were, I wasn't.

When I awoke each day
It took me a moment to realize
This strange sense of disorientation
Was me without you.

I could not tell you, or see you,
But I could feel you there,
You in your world, me in mine;
I couldn't bridge the veil of life.

Powerless to shift it,
To share it with you, came also
The realization of life going on
In our separate worlds.

The veil of life is thin,
But you can't see through it.
You can't follow until it's time;
Until then, ask less of life.

Life has its own plan
And we are merely players.
Divided by all that we do not know,
We say our worldly prayers.

Moment of Despair

Once again I am
Back to the sabotage,
Back to the wasteland
Of self-doubt,
The montage of monotony,
The inability to move.
All energy has left me;
The spirits have fled,
The scene of disaster left,
No evidence to be found,
All strength and empowerment gone.
Where? Was it ever truly there?
Did any of it really exist?
Under sunless January skies,
Melancholy and a cold wind,
Around a motherless child's cries,
All belief is gone now,
Disappeared into a wilderness.
Oh, Lord, why have you forsaken me?

The Psychic Tells Me: A Letter to Mother

Dear Mother,

They tell me you are an angel now and that no one was more surprised than you. The psychic checked out all of the details with me just to be sure! When she asked, "Did she touch a lot of lives?" I knew it was you.

Well, you sure did find your angel - even got your own set of wings. Is that like getting your first Indian feather? I always loved the angel ad on TV where she is eating Philadelphia cream cheese with 'her man' and getting crumbs all over her wings. It will have new meaning now and remind me of you. I miss you.

The psychic tells me it is so rare going straight into the angel realms, so I guess there is hope for us all, then - something to aspire to. Or perhaps it is best if you don't aspire at all. You kind of either get there or you don't!

Here I was trying to light your way through Bardot with a candle and you were already zooming up there in time for angelic tea. How like you! All that worry for nothing! Did I do a good job on our eulogy, Mother? I hope somebody does the same for me. And yes, I will try not to doubt like you did. I intend to keep my own faith. But I am not as good as I was, with nobody to jolly me on.

They tell me that your high frequency makes it hard for me to 'feel' you or sense you. I am glad that you are an angel, Mother, but could you not have been more like everybody else? Don't answer that - I know. The psychic tells me you will practise emerging on my birthday, perhaps as a ball of light before me in June. She tells me that I will still not be sure of what I see. Better get working on those vibrations, Mother - you know I will need a sign no smaller than the burning bush; I am like doubting Thomas.

I have been thinking that if you are this angel, how are we ever going to be together again? I don't think we can aspire to your level Mother, and we may have a few more rounds of the life circuit yet. What if our vibrations don't mesh with yours? There are so many 'what ifs' that life is beginning to seem simpler than death.

Thank you for sending the new babies and the weddings – we know you had a hand in that. Just to keep us all busy by creating a distraction or two! We really do need a lot of help down here. It's like living in the midst of chaos, what with disease, wars and famine. Things don't improve at all, but I guess you know that.

Mother, I have tried to piece it all together, to find you, but it makes me too sad and I have to let go. All the eons of time and space are behind us and before us; our past, present and future lives we carry with us deep within our soul.

I miss you,

Love always.

Dad

As I reflect on times gone by
I rarely heard you question why,
Accepting all in your quiet way.

Sometimes it seems to me
That you must be the wisest dad
A daughter ever had,
Not proud, or grand,
But real enough to lend a hand;
With not too much ambition
You always had the clearest vision.

You taught me how to paint
And how to make a garden grow;
You taught me almost everything I know -
How to fish, to rustle up a dish.
You tried to fill my every wish.

Deliberating wisely on plans
You took things calm and slow,
Made time to watch the flowers grow.
No need to go so fast -
You made the simple pleasures last.

December was your birth sign,
Though it did not suit you well,
Often under another spell.
You were my kind, understanding dad;
It took a lot to make you mad.

You never talked much about your past.
It seemed at times you carried weight –
Perhaps it was childhood fate?
A brother who had drowned?
A father who had frowned?

You always kept me grounded,
But liked to travel and be away
More than you could say.
Our midnight understanding talks
Led me on many paths and forks.

I thank you for your guidance,
Your wise council and your care
For the large, gentle hands of father bear,
Leaving a legacy to share.
You left your love, everywhere.

Painting

My space and comfort zone
Is there at my command.
I can bring to life a canvas
With the paint in my hand.

I can wash away a grey day
And make the flowers grow.
I can bring to life a place
That only I might know.

Life awash with colour,
I have no need, or care,
And you are bringing tea
But I didn't see you there.

Now I hear you calling
Somewhere in my head,
But I am slave to cause
When it becomes time for bed.

I can return again and again
To the gift of simple ways –
Painting is a joy of my life,
A gift of many happy days.

Ah, Grandchildren!

Ah, grandchildren!
The delight of life –
They will get you through
Both the joy and the strife.
They will remind you
Of all those forgotten things.
Their words will touch you
Like a thousand angels' wings.
The serious little sorrows
Are your remembrance
Of yesterday and tomorrow.
All the laughter, coaxing and pain
Make you relive it all again.
You are there to encourage
And to simplify it all.
There is no more noble calling
Than the grandparent call.
They will show you
How much fun life is
To live and live again.
When they are stuffed with love
You can send them home then.